AURORAS

Lisa Bullard

childsworld.com

Published by The Child's World®
800-599-READ • www.childsworld.com

Copyright © 2025 by The Child's World®
All rights reserved. No part of this book may be reproduced or utilized in any form or by any means without written permission from the publisher.

Photography Credits
Photographs ©: Kent Miller/National Park Service, cover, 1, 18; Sean Neilson/National Park Service, 2–3; Susan M. Snyder/Shutterstock Images, 5; Ross Burgener/NOAA, 6; Alex Gerst/NASA, 9; NASA, 11; Sanka Vidanagama/NurPhoto/Getty Images, 12; Jacob Frank/National Park Service, 15; Mark Stacey/NOAA, 16; J. Nichols/ESA/NASA, 20; Jacob W. Frank/National Park Service, 21

ISBN Information
9781503894396 (Reinforced Library Binding)
9781503895133 (Portable Document Format)
9781503895959 (Online Multi-user eBook)
9781503896772 (Electronic Publication)

LCCN 2024942894

Printed in the United States of America

ABOUT THE AUTHOR
Lisa Bullard is the author of more than 100 books for children, including the mystery novel *Turn Left at the Cow*. She also teaches writing classes for adults and children. Lisa grew up in Minnesota and now lives just north of Minneapolis.

CONTENTS

CHAPTER ONE
NATURE'S AMAZING LIGHT SHOW ... 4

CHAPTER TWO
COLLISIONS IN EARTH'S ATMOSPHERE ... 8

CHAPTER THREE
WHERE AND WHEN TO SEE AURORAS ... 14

Glossary ... 22
Fast Facts ... 23
One Stride Further ... 23
Find Out More ... 24
Index ... 24

CHAPTER ONE

NATURE'S AMAZING LIGHT SHOW

Alex walks out of his home in Fairbanks, Alaska, to stare up into the moonless midnight sky. The winter air is cold, but Alex knows the show will be worth it. A greenish haze glows faintly along the northern horizon. Alex watches as beams of green light stretch upward. They expand. The color shifts and shimmers. It ranges from the soft yellow green of new leaves to a bright lime color. Then a band of bright pink washes across the dark. It dips and sways alongside the greens. Intense waves of color now consume the dark sky overhead, rippling like curtains fluttering in a breeze. Hints of blue and purple flicker in and out. The dancing colors swirl and shimmy.

The best time to see auroras in Alaska is between late August and mid-April.

The aurora australis is visible in the southern hemisphere, including over Antarctica.

After about 15 minutes, the colors grow more muted. They blink out into a green mist. The mist slowly fades until the sky is dark and clear. Alex heads back to bed, only a little disappointed that the amazing display is over. After all, he knows it will return another night soon.

This eruption of color is not the result of a human-made light show. It is not a special effect created for a movie about an alien invasion. Instead, it is a natural **phenomenon** called the aurora (uh-ROR-uh). It is also known as the polar lights. In some locations, this vibrant show takes place more than half the nights of the year.

In the northern **hemisphere**, these lights are known as the aurora borealis (bor-ee-AL-iss). They are also called the northern lights. People in parts of Alaska and countries close to the northern polar region see them fairly often. This includes parts of Canada, Norway, and Iceland.

In the southern hemisphere, this phenomenon is called the aurora australis (ah-STRA-liss). Another name for it is the southern lights. The aurora australis lights up the night in places such as Tasmania, New Zealand, and Antarctica. These are all locations in or near the southern polar region.

There are times when people farther away from the poles can see auroras, too. It all depends on something that happens 93 million miles (150 million km) away. Auroras are caused by activity on the Sun's surface.

CHAPTER TWO

COLLISIONS IN EARTH'S ATMOSPHERE

Activity on the Sun's surface causes space weather. This weather affects the rest of the solar system. The Sun is a ball of superhot gases. These gases are made up of **particles** charged with electricity. Some of these particles shoot into space at high speeds. This is called the solar wind. Solar wind can reach Earth's **atmosphere** in about two to four days.

Earth's atmosphere is surrounded by an invisible shield called the magnetosphere. This protects the Earth from most of the solar wind. If there were no shield, the fast-moving solar wind would damage Earth's atmosphere. The solar wind is strong enough to change the shape of the shield around Earth. On the side of the Earth that faces the Sun, the wind pushes against the shield. The shield stretches out on the side facing away from the Sun, so it looks like a tail.

Auroras are visible from space.

Earth's core is made up mostly of iron. That means Earth itself acts like a huge magnet. The two ends of a magnet are called the **magnetic poles**. Earth's magnetic poles shift around. Despite this movement, one of them is somewhere near the true geographic North Pole. That is the northernmost part of Earth. Earth's other magnetic pole is somewhere near the true geographic South Pole. That is the southernmost part of Earth.

Part of the magnetosphere is a magnetic field around Earth. Sometimes particles of solar wind become trapped in Earth's magnetic field. This introduces extra energy into the magnetic field. Charged particles from the magnetic field move toward the magnetic poles and into Earth's atmosphere.

Earth's atmosphere is made up of gases. Nitrogen and oxygen are the two most common. The charged particles crash into these gases. This creates bursts of light. As billions of bursts take place, the lights seem to move. These colorful light shows are called auroras. **Auroral ovals** form in the atmosphere above and loosely centered around Earth's two magnetic poles.

HOW AURORAS FORM

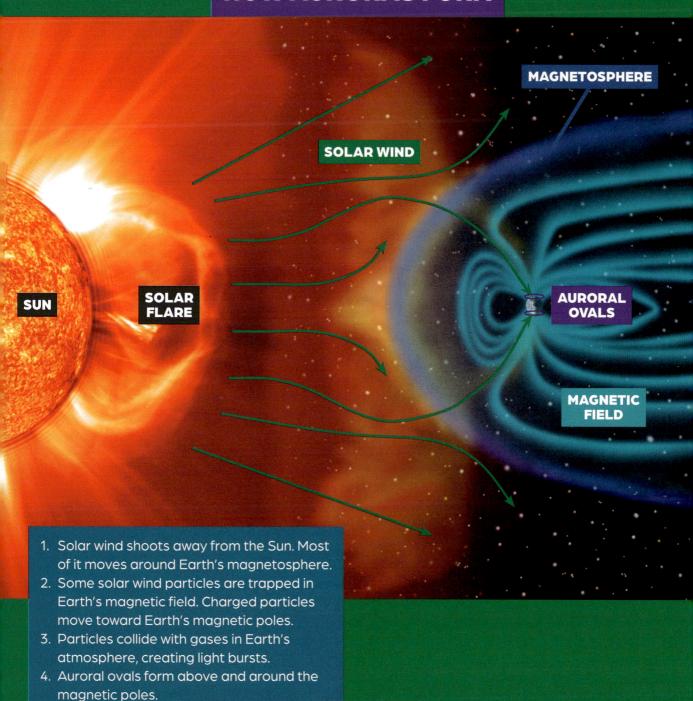

1. Solar wind shoots away from the Sun. Most of it moves around Earth's magnetosphere.
2. Some solar wind particles are trapped in Earth's magnetic field. Charged particles move toward Earth's magnetic poles.
3. Particles collide with gases in Earth's atmosphere, creating light bursts.
4. Auroral ovals form above and around the magnetic poles.

An aurora australis display over New Zealand shows an impressive range of colors. These colors are caused by different gases in Earth's atmosphere.

Auroras appear in many different colors. The colors are partly determined by which gas the particles collide with. Colors are also determined by how high above Earth's surface the collision happens. The most common aurora color is green. That is partly because human eyes see green better than other colors, especially at night. The green color is caused when particles collide with oxygen close to Earth. Oxygen collisions that happen higher up cause a red color. Blues and purplish reds are caused by collisions with nitrogen. Sometimes the colors seem only white to the human eye. The different colors may also mix to create colors such as pink and yellow. There may be other colors that human eyes cannot see.

AURORAS AND TECHNOLOGY ISSUES

Space weather and the auroras it creates can cause problems with technology. Radio and TV broadcasts can be disrupted. Radar signals, which are used to track things such as airplanes, might have issues. The systems that provide electricity can go down, leading to power outages. Satellites and navigation tools such as GPS can also be affected.

CHAPTER THREE

WHERE AND WHEN TO SEE AURORAS

Auroras happen on a regular basis. They take place even when people cannot see them. But when auroras are *happening* is not the same thing as when auroras are *visible*. There are certain factors that make it more likely to see an aurora. Two of the biggest considerations are place and time.

People located near an auroral oval have the best chance of seeing an aurora. For example, Fairbanks, Alaska, is located right under an auroral oval. During certain times of year, people in Fairbanks might see auroras on four out of five clear nights. Auroras are also sometimes visible in other areas of the United States, especially in the northern parts of states such as Minnesota, Michigan, and Maine.

The aurora borealis is sometimes visible at Glacier National Park in Montana.

Space weather is always changing. Solar storms mean more intense auroras. The auroral ovals also expand. Auroras might be seen in places even farther away from the poles. Extreme solar activity has even triggered visible auroras in Mexico.

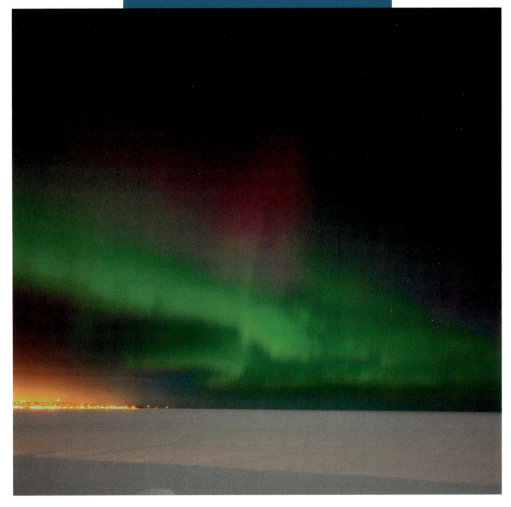

An aurora borealis display lights up the sky over Lake Superior in Michigan.

Sunspots are one kind of solar activity that affect auroras. Sunspots are the coldest parts of the Sun. They cause bursts of energy in the solar wind. The number of sunspots varies in a cycle of about 11 years. For about the first half of those 11 years, the number of sunspots increases to a high peak. For around the second half, the number decreases. Then the cycle repeats. As each cycle heads toward the peak, auroras usually become more intense and visible in more places. Solar Cycle 25 began in 2019. Scientists cannot identify the highest peak of a cycle until months after it has happened. But they can make **predictions**. Researchers predicted Cycle 25's peak would be in 2024 or 2025.

In Alaska, the Sun does not fully set in the summers. The sky is too bright for people to see auroras during that time.

Auroras are not equally visible in all seasons. In places near the poles, the Sun never sets on some summer nights. Nights get longer as the seasons turn from fall to winter. Auroras are more likely to be seen in seasons when nights are longer. The periods near the spring and fall **equinoxes** offer good chances for aurora viewing. The way the Earth is tilted at those times of year means more solar wind gets into Earth's magnetic field.

Auroras can take place at any time, day or night. But they are visible only when it is dark out. People are most likely to see them between 10 p.m. and 2 a.m.

Scientists have found ways to predict how likely it is that auroras will be visible. Some factors are easy to track. For example, the light of a full moon might interfere with aurora viewing. The moon's cycles are known and predictable. Other factors are harder to predict. The sky might cloud over unexpectedly. Space weather could change. But scientists can measure the solar wind using satellites. They can program computers to predict when people are most likely to see auroras in different locations. Some organizations post their aurora predictions. These organizations include the US government's Space Weather Prediction Center and the Australian Space Weather Forecasting Centre.

AURORAS IN OUTER SPACE

Auroras are not just a phenomenon on Earth. Other planets and moons in the solar system have auroras, too. Scientists have even discovered a comet with auroras. They have also found evidence that auroras happen outside the solar system. Some of these auroras are very different from Earth's. For example, Jupiter's auroras are especially powerful. But most of the light is not visible to human eyes. Some telescopes on Earth can see **ultraviolet** (UV) light, allowing scientists to see auroras that would not usually be visible to humans.

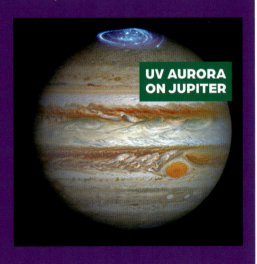

UV AURORA ON JUPITER

Seeing an aurora is never a guarantee. But people can improve their chances. They can check scientific predictions. They can travel closer to an auroral oval. They can choose a time and location where the sky is likely to be dark and clear. They can travel away from city lights. Even taking all those things into account, however, people may also need to be patient. But whether because of scientific predictions or a happy accident, some lucky people will be fortunate enough to see an aurora at some point in their lives.

An aurora is an incredible sight for people lucky enough to see one.

GLOSSARY

atmosphere (AT-muss-feer) An atmosphere is the layer of gases that surrounds a planet. Collisions in Earth's atmosphere lead to bursts of light called auroras.

auroral ovals (uh-ROR-uhl OH-vullz) The auroral ovals are two ring-shaped areas in Earth's atmosphere that are loosely centered on Earth's magnetic poles. The auroral ovals are where aurora activity takes place, and they expand during solar storms.

equinoxes (EE-kwuh-nahk-sez) Equinoxes are the times in spring and fall when day and night are the same length. Auroras are often very active around the spring and fall equinoxes.

hemisphere (HEM-iss-feer) A hemisphere is half of a round object. Earth has a northern hemisphere and a southern hemisphere.

magnetic poles (mag-NET-ik POLLZ) Magnetic poles are the two ends of a magnet. Earth has two magnetic poles, a North Pole and a South Pole.

particles (PAR-tih-kullz) Particles are tiny parts of something. Solar wind is made up of particles from the Sun.

phenomenon (fuh-NAH-muh-nahn) A phenomenon is an observable event that can be explained by science. An aurora is a colorful phenomenon that can be seen in the night sky.

predictions (prih-DIK-shunz) Predictions are guesses about what will happen in the future based on observation or experience. Scientists cannot say for sure when auroras will be visible, but they can make predictions.

ultraviolet (ull-truh-VYE-uh-lit) Ultraviolet light is light just outside of what humans can see. Jupiter's auroras can be in ultraviolet light.

FAST FACTS

✸ An aurora is a natural phenomenon that features colorful displays of light in the night sky.

✸ The aurora borealis (northern lights) happens mostly in areas close to the North Pole. The aurora australis (southern lights) happens mostly in areas close to the South Pole.

✸ Auroras begin with solar winds shooting away from the Sun. Most of the solar winds flow around Earth's magnetosphere, but some particles are trapped in the magnetic field.

✸ Particles collide with gases in Earth's atmosphere and bursts of color are released.

✸ Sometimes solar storms lead to auroras farther away from the poles.

✸ People are more likely to see auroras in fall through spring, at times of increased sunspots, and on dark, clear nights.

ONE STRIDE FURTHER

✸ What are some of the other effects that the Sun has on Earth?

✸ Have you ever seen an aurora? How would you describe it to a friend?

✸ Of the countries or states mentioned in the book, which one would you most like to visit for an aurora trip? Why?

✸ When people saw auroras in the time before science had an explanation for this phenomenon, what kind of stories do you imagine they told about these amazing light displays?

FIND OUT MORE

IN THE LIBRARY

Allan, Sophie. *The Solar System: Discover the Mysteries of Our Sun and Neighboring Planets*. New York, NY: DK Publishing, 2023.

Allen, Stacy. *Rainbows and Halos*. Parker, CO: The Child's World, 2025.

Smith, Jennifer N. R. *Bang: The Wild Wonders of Earth's Phenomena*. New York, NY: Thames & Hudson, 2024.

ON THE WEB

Visit our website for links about auroras:

childsworld.com/links

Note to Parents, Caregivers, Teachers, and Librarians: We routinely verify our web links to make sure they are safe and active sites. So encourage your readers to check them out!

INDEX

atmosphere, 8–10, 11
aurora australis, 7
aurora borealis, 7

colors, 4–7, 10, 13

equinoxes, 18

gases, 8, 10, 11, 13

Jupiter, 20

magnetic field, 10, 11, 18
magnetosphere, 8–10, 11

Solar Cycle 25: 17
solar wind, 8–10, 11, 17–19
Sun, 7, 8, 11, 17–18
sunspots, 17

technology, 13
tips for viewing, 18–20

where to see auroras, 4, 7, 14–16